Unleash Your SuperPower!

6 extraordinary stories on discovering and accepting the power within

Compiled by: Lisa Dove Washington

COMPILED BY: Lisa Dove Washington © 2019

ALL RIGHTS RESERVED. No part of this book may be reproduced in any written, electronic, recording, or photocopying without written permission of the publisher or author. The exception would be in the case of brief quotations embodied in the critical articles or reviews and pages where permission is specifically granted by the publisher or author.

PUBLISHED BY: Touched By A Dove Publishing
TYPESETTING & LAYOUT BY: Junnita Jackson
(www.theliarscraft.com)
STORY EDITING BY: Co-Authors

DISCLAIMER
Although you may find the teachings, life lessons and examples in this book to be useful, the book is sold with the understanding that neither the co-authors nor Touched By A Dove Publishing. are engaged in presenting any legal, relationship, financial, emotional, or health advice.

Any person who's experiencing financial, anxiety, depression, health, or relationship issues should consult with a licensed therapist, advisor, licensed psychologist, or any qualified professional before commencing into anything described in this book. This book's intent is to provide you with the writer's account and experience with overcoming life matters. All results will differ; however, our goal is to provide you with our "take" on how to overcome and be resilient when faced with circumstances. There are lessons in every blessing.

ISBN: 978-0-578-53187-8
PRINTED IN THE UNITED STATES OF AMERICA.

Contents

Introduction
1

Chapter 1   Rev. DR. J. L. Brown Jr.
7

Chapter 2   Maria Thorpe
19

Chapter 3   Antwan Brown
29

Chapter 4   Tawawn Lowe
43

Chapter 5   Lisa Dove Washington
55

Chapter 6   Quashon Davis
67

Introduction

Unleash Your SuperPower: 6 Extraordinary Stories on Discovering and Accepting the Power Within is a collection of short stories from extraordinary people bonding together to inspire you to discover what your Superpower is and how to accept the responsibility that comes along with it. Learning to do something that you never thought you wanted to do, needed to do, or even could do and then conquering it, is the kind of SuperPower that we want to tap into in the book. These six dynamic writers have overcome self-sabotaging thoughts, fear, failure, and procrastination in order to discover their ability to achieve the impossible. They've paid their dues, owned their stories, and excited to share their playbook on how they were able to tap into their powers to create a life full of wealth, happiness, peace, and excellence. So, if you are ready to discover, unleash, and execute a new reality, this book is for you.

Now let's get those capes ready because it's time for the Superhero in you to shine through. UNLEASH your Superpowers!!! Life is full of challenges, good and bad, and we all wish we had that special gift, magic wand, or "Superpower" that would make it all right or make it all go away. Well, I am here to tell you that that particular Superpower you are looking for probably doesn't exist, BUT, there is a Superpower that does and it's all yours. The work is in figuring out what it is and how to use it. This book will help you and others learn how to discover what your specific Superpower is and learn how to accept all that comes with it. Having a Superpower is not all roses and it is not all fun either. Just like Superman, who could do all kinds of things that normal people couldn't, he also had things that challenged him with those powers. There were things that he had to stay away from, or it would affect his powers and abilities. Your Superpowers work the same way. There will be gifts that are yours, created and given specifically to you and as you discover them, you will also realize that there will be consequences to having them and using them.

Have you ever experienced something in life and in the aftermath, you wondered how you ever got through it? How did you get through the fire and still stand tall? Have you ever been through something that challenged everything within you, your beliefs, your heart, your trust, your fears, and through the trials and tribulations, you started to feel empowered by the journey? That is the moment that you are coming into an understanding and discovering your superpower. Discovering your superpower and learning to accept how pivotal it is in embracing the challenges that you will come across in life on a daily basis will be hard at times but definitely doable. The more we learn about ourselves and what makes us tick, the more ready we are to take on what comes our way.

By taking charge of your next steps and learning what your Superpowers (gifts) are, you are one step closer to understanding who you are and how you show up in this world we live in. When you stop and think about it, we have a lot in common with the superheroes we know and love! For Example: Superman's strengths are flight, x-ray vision, heat vision, cold breath, super-speed, enhanced hearing but his weaknesses are high gravity, a red sun, majic and Kryptonite. Wonder Woman's strengths are superhuman strength, durability, the power of flight, reflexes, agility and enhanced senses, including smell. She also had these powerful bracelets, that if stolen or lost or even tied together, would cause her to go into an uncontrollable rage. The Wolverine's strengths are superhuman strength, animal-keen senses and regeneration ability (healing power) and his metal skeleton that actually leads to one of his weakness which is magnets. And although he has an amazing healing power that protects him and makes even poisoning him very difficult, with the right dosage, it can take him out. Cat Woman's superpowers are street fighting and martial arts, cat-like speed, reflexes, balance and flexibility but did you know that her weakness is her sense of duty and her obligations of the police and vigilantes? And finally, is the Black Panther who holds powers of healing, invisibility, teleportation, walking on water and super strength as well as a genius level of intellect but he has weaknesses that challenge those powers like arrogance, magic, strong Nationalism and daddy issues. All these Superheroes possess superpowers (strengths, gifts) that helped them to save the world and do good things, but not one of them were all powerful. Many of their superpowers could be lost through their weaknesses and vulnerabilities. Did you notice that many of them shared the same superpowers or even had the same weakness as some of you may have? Interesting, huh? I thought so too. Everyone has things that are considered to be their gifts. And we have things that will cause us to either lose those gifts or weaken their strengths. It is up to us to know what they are so that we can put our best foot forward in everything we do. The idea for this book came about because I know that we all are on a journey in this life. Discovering our personal superpowers and accepting what comes with them is a big part of the journey. We sometimes make decisions and do things that can jeopardize those gifts, strengths and talents because we don't know what they are or how to protect them. I mentioned the superheroes above to show how we can all possess some of the same strengths while also sharing some of the same weaknesses. Why not use this book to help people learn how to discover the inner strengths and learn how to accept the good, the bad and the ugly that go along with it? Do you know or have an idea of what your Superpowers are? Do you ever think about the challenges that come with them? Let's work toward discovering them together.

The Unleash Your Superpower Crew

"SUPERPOWERS"

<u>Rev. Dr. J. L. Brown</u>
Superpower - Faith & Determination

<u>Tawawn Lowe</u>
Superpower - Untying the Knots

<u>Antwan Brown</u>
Superpower – Mental Strength

<u>Maria Thorpe</u>
Superpower – PAID
(Positive Attitude & Intense Determination)

<u>Lisa Dove Washington</u>
Superpower – Forgiveness

<u>Quashon Davis</u>
Superpower – Healing & Recovery

Rev. DR. J. L. Brown Jr.

    At twenty-five years of age, Joseph L. Brown, Jr. was living on top of the world – he had it all. Ten years later, it was all gone, including his dignity. When he reached the bottomless pit, he recognized that the Lord giveth and the Lord taketh away. He has always wanted to help others but, it wasn't until he met Christ in the pit that he rose to the servant that he is today by serving those in need.

    From birth, it was known that he was blessed with the spirit of kindness and love. His proud mother always sings praises to God for blessing her with a humble son that always thinks of others before thinking of himself. His family affectionately call him the caregiver.

He is a 1985 graduate of H.D. Woodson High School a.k.a. The Warriors. He played the clarinet and was a proud member of the "Warrior Marching Band". Joseph was known in school as the guy who had that swag and that would keep you laughing.

He was licensed to preach God's word among the Baptist faith in 1990 and ordained as a Baptist Minister in 2013. Rev. Brown received his Bachelor of Theology in 2015 and plans to receive a Masters of Theology in the spring of 2020 from Andersonville Theological Seminary. Humble and honored, he will receive his Doctorate in Human Letters from Trinity International University of Ambassadors in September 2019.

Rev. Brown is bi-vocational. He is a Master Heating, Ventilation, Air Conditioning and Refrigeration Contractor and a DC First Class Steam Engineer servicing the tristate areas of the District, Maryland and Virginia.

Rev. Brown is the proud father of two daughters; Skye Olivia and Destiny Alexis. They are both artistic in their own right.

Rev. Brown is an avid sports enthusiast who loves to spend time cheering for his favorite football team, the Pittsburgh Steelers. He also loves relaxing and enjoying a good comedy or suspense movie.

Driven to succeed, Rev. Brown has several upcoming projects that he is devoted to mastering and completing so that he can continue to help others succeed. Soaring like an eagle, he gives all praises to God for bringing him to this point in his life. Stay tuned to hear more about how God's loving grace and mercy continues to bless Rev. Joseph Lamar Brown, Jr., so that he can continue to bless others.

I WANT IT ALL BACK!

I often wondered what it would feel like to be an outcast. To go days without food or water. How would my body feel? What would it be like to go weeks without having a conversation with your family? Even worse, what it would feel like not talking to anyone about anything. I was wondering, thinking about the life of someone homeless.

I didn't have to wonder anymore. I was homeless.

I was standing in a long line to get something to eat for the day. I gazed at the blue sky and asked Him (God) why? Why was I here - hungry and thirsty? Why was I waiting in a line, not at a grocery store or at a restaurant, for something to eat and drink? I was waiting for food without giving money. I was expecting to get something to eat and drink, but not the way that I was used to getting it. Everything changed when I became homeless. I slept in one abandoned car after another. It didn't matter if it were a Ford or a Chrysler. I also slept in vacant apartments in the complex that I once lived. I just needed some place to lay my head.

I could not believe it. I had nothing. I did not have a place to decorate to call home. There was no need to frequent a gas station because I no longer had a car. Other than the clothes on my back and one large trash bag of clothing, I did not have it. "It" was no longer a part of my life.

I went from having everything to having nothing.

All was lost, and it was all gone.

I lost hope. I lost it all!

You'll be surprised at the things you take for granted when you're homeless. I missed the warm beds during the winter and the cool breeze coming through my bedroom window during the summer. You have a different mindset when you are homeless. You shift into a survival mindset. Each day is just another day. The seasons never change when you are homeless, and the seasons come and go. There is not a weather report, but your body senses the weather day by day.

I was working in an apartment complex as an HVAC (Heating Ventilation and Air Conditioning) technician. As part of my payment for servicing the units, I was able to live in the complex. But I was late to appointments and sometimes I didn't show at all. As a result, I was fired and asked to vacate the premises. I didn't have a place to live. I didn't have any family that I could rely on at this time. I asked myself - where would I live? How will I eat and care for myself?

The solution to my homelessness? I chose to live in abandoned cars. There were several abandoned cars that I knew about while working in the apartment complex. Yes, I lost it all! Brokenness is often the road to a breakthrough. Be encouraged!

I had begun craving alcohol. That craving became my worst nightmare. It was an addiction that caused me to lose it all. I lost my job, my home, my communication with family and friends. I lost my hope. I lost me. I disappeared into the chains of oppression and despair. I lost my dreams, my aspirations. I lost it all!

Water, shelter and clothing were not just a necessity. It became a day-to-day challenge. I was poisoned. My mind was no longer mine. I was a victim. I was a victim of my circumstances. Because of my troubles, I felt like I no longer had a purpose.

Life is based on choices. The choices that we or someone else makes for us determines our destiny. I had allowed my alcohol addiction to guide me in the decisions that I was making. Family and friends were convinced that if I moved from a certain location and I did not have certain people around me, that I would not be influenced to drink alcohol. For me taking the location and the people away only enhanced my desire to drink. My life was like a chess game being played at the speed of a ping pong game. Sometimes God will let you hit rock bottom so that you will discover that He is the rock on the bottom.

While waiting in the line at the soup kitchen, my mind wandered more. Why was I here at rock bottom? I knew better. I wasn't raised this way. When did my world begin to unravel? I had a decent job leading towards a promising career. I had a nicely decorated place to live and family and friends to share a few laughs. I hear my inner voice telling me who I am. Who am I?

You are unique. You are secret to your own success. You are respectful. You are Joseph L, Brown, Jr. You are an example for your children. Yes, you are an example for other children.

You make great choices. You are great at every little thing that you try to do. You do beautiful work. People always rely and call on you. You are highly recommended. You are Joe Brown the Top Shelf Engineer.

You are extraordinary. You earn the respect of others. You are a driving force. You are the helper in the family. You are Joey the son, the brother, the uncle.

You are a pleasure to know. You are the good seed that keeps on growing and growing and growing. You give out great advice and you are always helping someone – even strangers. You are Mr. Brown.

You are happy. You are full of life. You are joy. You are an excellent preacher and teacher. You study God's word and pray without ceasing. You have a heart for people, and you let your little light shine and you draw people to Christ. You are Rev. Joseph L. Brown, Jr. Hold up! Wait A Minute! Who Are You?

At that moment, I recognized that I was no longer that man, the man I know I could be. Who had I become? The man that ran away. The man that could not and would not stay. The champ that gave away his identity. The rock that crushed his own integrity. The powerhouse that dropped everything to gain nothing. The reflection of pity. The outstanding great hero who was failing his own test.

I realized that I had it all and now I had nothing...nothing but hopelessness. I am an alcoholic. I have drunk everything, and I do mean everything until I could not drink anymore. I needed an answer to the question - now that I have hit rock bottom, how can I get it all back? That was the question!

As I wallowed in my own sweat, at my own pity party, like the prodigal son I knew that I was bigger than this. I thought back to my church days and remembered the scripture - I lift up my eyes to the hills. From where does my help come? My help comes from the LORD (Psalm 121:1-2). I remembered a sermon that I preached that focused on giving my best and communicating with God. I knew I had a purpose in life. I remembered that before I was born, God knew me and my purpose. The life that I was now living was not my purpose. Another scripture resonated with my spirit. Psalm 37:24 reads "Though he may stumble, he will not fall for the Lord upholds him with his hand."

The Warrior Mentality

I fought against the devil using the wrong weapons. I tried to think logically and systematically. I had an answer for each scenario and each analogy. Before I left Maryland, I moved from my home to go live with relatives. I was a mess. I had several friends and a few relatives try relentlessly to bring me back to my senses. It did not work. I listened but that was about it. Through intervention methods, my frat brothers tried to prevent me from drinking alcohol. It did not work. A cousin brought me from one cousin's home in Maryland to live with her in Virginia. She worked with me until I got up on my feet with a nice job and was able to eventually pride myself in my own place. The demands of the job became an excuse and eventually I began to drink again. Then a friend from the past convinced me that the sunshine state of Florida was the relaxing place to be. He had a job lined up in an apartment building for me and I could live there for a reduced fee. I was there for a short time but once again, drinking alcohol uncontrollably became a way of life for me. I was addicted. I was an alcoholic.

At first, I did not know I had a problem. When family would pour the alcohol down the drain and when frat brothers would plan an intervention and when close friends would plead their case, I could not see it then. I had a problem. I was the problem. I needed to find a way to resolve the problem. I eventually discovered that there is a super-power that you must have to do anything in life. FAITH AND DETERMINATION will help you accomplish your goal and should become a way of life. It has for me in everything that I do. Cast all your worries on the Lord. He cares for you (1 Peter 5:7). With my faith in God, I was determined that alcohol was not going to define me. Alcohol was not going to rule me. Alcohol was not going to determine where I would work or where I would live. Alcohol would not determine who I would talk to and would not keep me away from God. This would not be the end of my story.

    I wanted to and needed to fix my life. I sought help from family as I moved from Florida to South Carolina. Like the prodigal son, I wanted to come back home to family. With the assistance of relatives, I entered an outpatient program, but I knew I had to make up in my mind that the only way to a victorious lifestyle was to have the mindset of self-preservation. With faith I was determined to beat the addicted lifestyle that I knew and to be the best that I could at everything that I do.

    I thought about it. I spent most of my time drinking instead of working. Drinking became a part of me and everything in my life centered around drinking. I had to admit it and then do something about it. I convinced myself that I was better than a bottle and that I was better than a habit.

    When you are homeless, people really ignore you. I never was one that begged for money but somehow, I managed to work enough at a day labor job where I would have just enough to get me a drink or two. Sometimes you meet people who are in the same situation as you and you feel a magnet drawing you to them. But for the better good in me, I became determined while in that soup kitchen line in Florida and in South Carolina that I was going to beat this ugly habit. I was determined and had faith.

Other than a few people who were in my circle, no one would speak to me or carry on a conversation with me. You become dehumanized and the people around you are in the same mindset as you. So, you don't think positive and you only have a one-track mind – when will I get my next drink. Because of my troubles, I no longer felt like I had a purpose. At the time I did not realize that the challenges that I met were a part of the process. The process itself was all in the mind. I needed to go through this for myself.

Jesus commanded me to leave my old ways and He told me that He would make way for a new creature – a new me. No longer in self-pity, I am determined to beat the storms of life by showing love and kindness to my fellow man.

After the out-patient program, I decided to come back to my roots in the Washington DC area. I began to study relentlessly God's word. I enrolled in school and I now have my Bachelor's and Master of Theology and soon a PhD. Also, during the 12 years of being sober, I obtained my Master HVAC Licenses in Maryland, Washington, DC and Virginia. I also obtained my DC First Class Steam Engineer License. I have secured several jobs in my career that have made me and my family proud to say the least. I was determined to keep my faith in God and to do the right things for me and my family.

As the song states Bridge Over Troubled Waters, I have seen the sun shining as darkness has filled me but with determination as my key, I have overcome. When going through I am sure people were there for me but because of my addiction, I felt as though no one was there. I had to make the connection or go over the bridge from trouble waters (alcohol addiction) to little victories to a bigger success story. I started small and celebrated each little victory. You are fearfully and wonderfully made. What God has for you it is for you and no one can hinder the blessings of God.

I discovered God's purpose for my life. Success comes from getting back up again and again and again. As God sees your efforts, He will guide you to victory. You may face roadblocks. But God will allow you to climb those mountains or He will knock them down for you. A prayer unanswered may be a blessing delayed. God knows when you are ready for your blessings and He will allow you to walk into them with faith and determination.

God is not finished with me. I'm not perfect. But I try to live a Christ-like life. I have a great career, family by my side and friends that I can count on, but nothing equates to the relationship that I have with God. He has prevented me from many dangers and allowed me to go through the storm. I have bumps and bruises but through this well-groomed body that the Lord has blessed me with, I know that it could have been the other way. I could be the one out there sleeping in a car and not knowing where my next meal was coming from. I was that person.

I have buried the desire for alcohol and have gone to bearing the desire for the living water. Jesus is the foundation. He is the rock. I collapsed but I did not falter. The rock did not cave in. I remembered where I came from and whose I was. I remembered myself. I remembered the real Joseph L. Brown, Jr. But God really had to deal with me. I accepted the call to preach but ran from it. I'm so glad that God allowed me to think and to recognize His goodness and

His mercy is all that I need to live my life. I am no longer in captivity or in prison to the alcohol demon. Drinking and becoming homeless is real. I walked in the shoes of a homeless man who drank. I will never look at a homeless person or a person who has an addiction the same as I had before. My mission is to be the best that I can at all that I do and to help someone along the way. Who am I to judge?

For over 8 years I was judged. I am in no position to judge a person, but perhaps I am able to help that person see God's love. I have been there and done that. I am able to see and use the supernatural powers of God through faith and determination to get everything back that I lost. My Super-Powers – Faith and Determination

I don't have to compromise my beliefs because I know that my faith in God has caused me to be that determined man that will accomplish all there is for me to accomplish.

I have learned that I can't hold on to the past or problems. I am determined to not allow any poison to ruin my future. I am leaning towards greatness and not mediocracy. My faith will carry me through my bad days, and it is determination that will carry me through my bad days and good days. I have released the pains, hurts, and guilts of my wrongs. Claiming Your Inheritance

I am recommending the reader to do the faith challenge for 1 month. If you've had anything taken from you I challenge you to exercise faith. Now faith is being sure of what we hope for and certain of what we do not see. (Hebrews 11:1). You may not see a way to get what you lost, but faith says don't always trust what you see because God can turn nothing into something, a mess into a miracle, and life out of death. The challenge is for you to reclaim the things you lost and believe by faith that you will receive them. And when you incorporate determination into the challenge, it gives you more reason to work towards reclaiming your losses.

Once you concentrate daily on living by faith and NOT by sight, you will see your dreams and aspirations come true. Take that one step forward and don't look backwards. Leave all fears, negative thoughts and naysayers behind. Faith will not work if you don't put some action behind it. In other words, "Effort is demanded before a blessing can be handed". You can own that business, write that book, drive that car, get that degree and everything else in between. Your super-powers of faith and determination will carry you through the next dimension of success. Faith and Determination

If you have ever lost anything in your life, you can get it back! If the devil has stolen anything from you, you can get it back! However, you must want it back! You must really want it back! Your mind must be made up. You must have the assurance that you will be committed to do those things that are necessary to get it all back. With God everything is possible! He will give you all that you need to accomplish your task. If you want it all back and you have faith in God and are determined to do those things that are pleasing in His sight, He will see you through. Faith without works is dead. And you should never be lacking in zeal, but keep your spiritual fervor, serving the Lord. Be joyful in hope, patient in affliction, faithful in prayer. You can get it all back! Your peace and joy start from the head and then works down your entire being. Your mental, physical and spiritual self will prosper in everything that you do or say. You may be in an ugly place now but think with a mind of faith and be determined that you will come out of it.

Maria Thorpe

Engineer, Speaker, Mentor, Real Estate Investor an Agent, Business Owner, Mother, Wife, and Friend.

Maria Thorpe Is a native of Philadelphia Pa. and a graduate of the Philadelphia High School for Girls. She is a graduate of Leadership Southern MD, the Federal Executive Institute (FEI), National Defense University, Industrial College of the Armed Forces (ICAF) with a Master of Science in National Resource Strategy, Pennsylvania State University with a Master of Engineering, Engineering Science degree and a graduate of Drexel University, Philadelphia, PA with a Bachelor of Science in Electrical Engineering.

Ms. Thorpe is often a speaker at local schools and colleges on the topic of STEM. She has received numerous awards and honors, including but not limited to the following: Speaker at the STEM event, White House Day at the Labs, Carolyn E. Parker Foundation, Legacy Leader Award, Featured on the OCHR Website Employee Spotlight, Black Engineer of the Year Award for Community Service, Department of Defense Women's History Month STEM Role Model Award, Women of Color Technology & Defense Award for Outstanding Achievements in Government, and the Equal Employment Opportunity Honorary Award, for Excellence in Leadership. Ms. Thorpe is married to Roland Jr. and has two sons, Roland III and Malcolm, and currently resides in Southern MD.

PAID: A Path to Success!

I was born in Philadelphia, PA. I grew up in North Philly to be exact. The neighborhood was everything next to God and family. My mother had thirteen children but only eight survived. I am the youngest girl of eight children. My mother would always say to me and all of us, "I did not finish my high school education, but all my children will get a diploma." She believed that education was the key to success. My mom's goal for us made me determined to graduate from high school no matter what.

In this life we all have dreams, some big dreams when we are young. I would hear people say, "anything is possible if you work hard." But what they don't say is sometimes working hard is not enough. I have found that a critical part of success is having a positive attitude combined with intense determination. I like to call this the PAID Factor. I believe that GOD has given all of us some special powers. He does not come out and tell you what they are but they will manifest in special ways, in situations or in times of need. Sometimes it will exhibit itself when you are faced with a situation you think you can't handle. It is up to you to figure out what your superpower might be. My superpower manifested in a strength I call Positive Attitude with Intense Determination (PAID).

During my life I have found that having a positive attitude will put you in the correct frame of mind for whatever you want to do. Being able to keep a positive attitude during good and bad times is a must. Having determination will allow you to stay firm in your purpose. The dictionary defines determination as the process of establishing something exactly by calculation of research, the controlling or deciding of somethings nature or outcome, or firmness of purpose.

Over my life I have had to call upon this superpower often to meet my goals and the goals set before me by others. Let me share a story of how PAID was the key to my success.

I was educated in the Philadelphia school system and I had great teachers that allowed me to learn, grow and develop. My first recognized mentor was my elementary school teacher, Ms. Greene. She spent time showing me and sharing with me things I would have never seen otherwise. She would push me and there was no task that she gave me that I didn't do my best to exceed her expectations. She believed in me, so I believed in me too. She was one of the reasons that I was accepted into my high-achieving, academically challenging high school. She provided a recommendation for me to attend.

Senior year of High School. I made it. So many challenges, so many accomplishments. I was excited. I had worked hard to make sure to meet my mother's goal for all of her children to graduate from high school. During my senior year, there were various events I had to prepare for and lots of activities to participate in. However, at the beginning of this school year, a major event occurred. The city was gearing up for a major teacher strike. The strike began on September 8, 1981. Over 3500 teachers were being laid off because the school board had over a $220 million deficit. I had no idea how this would affect my senior year, but I knew the impact would be major. What was I going to do? This strike could affect my dreams of graduating and honoring my mother's wishes for her children to get their diploma.

The strike continued for days. There was concern from the parents and students about the impact of the strike on the school year. In an effort to keep the seniors on track and have them graduate on time, the school board decided that all seniors would go to school at least for part of the day so we would not fall behind in our academic requirements. The administration established what were called Senior Centers. A senior center was a local high school selected for a group of senior students who would attend that school to meet their educational requirements during the strike. Girls High School, my beloved high school was not on the list to be a senior High School Center, so I had to wait to see which school I would attend. I had no choice, my mother had no say in which school I would attend. It was decided by the school board administration.

I recall that there would only be a few high schools open to accommodate hundreds of students. Many of the students from my high school were sent to Germantown

High School as their senior center. I too was assigned to attend Germantown. This was a shock for many of us. The school was not in the best of neighborhoods and not the most academically challenging.

I didn't know much about this school or exactly where it was located. Once I found out where it was located, I had to find a way to get there. My family did not have a vehicle, so I would have to find a public transportation route or walk. I was determined to be positive about this situation. This was going to allow me to work on my requirements for graduation. I was not going to let this situation deter me from finishing my senior year.

I know that may sound simple, but it was not. There was not a direct route for me to get to this location easily by public transportation. It was going to add more time to an already early day. In addition, this would cost my family extra money, money we did not have, but I was determined to figure something out. I needed time to think. I retreated to my quiet place where I would not be disturbed. I had come to realize this is where my strength resides, in my solitude. I believe that your focus determines your reality and by the end of the day I had a plan. It was going to take a lot of effort on my part to make this happen, but I was determined to make this plan a reality.

I enlisted the help of my family and friends as I put a plan in place. My tribe was not going to let me fail at this challenge. They had just as much invested in this endeavor as I did. I was going places and they were determined to help me get there in any way they could.

I was up each morning at O' dark thirty. I got dressed and was ready for whatever the day would bring. Each morning I would walk to the subway several blocks away. I would catch the subway, then the trolley or sometimes just walk several more blocks to the senior center. I did this each day to and from the school.

Some students could not make it to these senior centers every day because it was just too much. However, with my plan in place I was able to get there every day of the strike. This allowed me to keep my perfect attendance record as well. I had a lot riding on graduating, and I was not going to let anything get in my way.

The school strike lasted for 50 days - the longest teacher strike we had ever seen - before the courts demanded the teachers return to work. I would soon be back at my own school continuing my stellar education as well as preparing for graduation.

I believed that all the drama was behind me and I would continue with all I had to do to complete my graduation requirements. However, there was more. Soon after the teacher strike ended, there was a public transportation strike! I took public transportation to school each day. Now I had yet another obstacle trying to prevent me from reaching my goal of graduating.

The subway was my form of transportation to school each day, and without it I would not be able to easily get to school. As I mentioned earlier, my family did not have a car that I could use so again I had to come up with a strategy to get me to school. This time it wouldn't be as easy as finding an alternative route to school. This was a special academic school I attended so it was not my neighborhood school. After talking with my family, my neighbors and friends again, I thought I had a plan that I could put into action. The strategy I had come up with would cause me to have to move out of my home. I would have to move in with another family that lived closer to my school.

This was only possible because, fortunately for me, my best friend growing up had moved a few years earlier, and where they moved was only a few miles from my high school. I called my best friend and told her about my idea. So of course, she thought this was a great idea too. It would give us a chance to spend more time together, because ever since she moved away, we had not had an opportunity to see each other. Next, I would have to convince my mother that this idea was plausible. I explained the situation to my mother and told her that my friends' mom would be calling. I had my best friend convinced her mother that this could work. Her mother called my mother and they agreed that the plan could work. I was allowed to stay at their home during the transportation strike. This was the first time I had ever lived away from my family.

My mother explained that I needed to be on my best behavior, to help around the house as much as possible but most of all be the young lady she had raised. I knew what that meant. She helped me pack and slipped a few dollars in my pocket for incidentals and off I went.

Even though my friends' home was closer to the school, I would still have to get up early and walk about 3 miles to get to school each day and then 3 miles back to their home in the evening. Sometimes I could get one of my friends to drop me off a few blocks away. At the end of each day, I had to do my schoolwork and help around the house. I was determined to graduate and if this was what I had to do then I was up for the challenge. I was so grateful to have the love and support of this family.

The transportation strike finally ended. I stayed at my friends' home until the end of the school week and returned home soon after.

I learned a lot about myself during this time and during this journey. I discovered what I called my five P's which helped me to express and /or develop my PAID superpower. They are: • Prioritize what is most important in your situation • Have Patience when things don't work the way you think they should • Persevere when doing something despite its difficulty • Persist in your course of action in spite of opposition, and • Be Positive. It will make the journey that much better. Between the teacher strike and the bus strike, my senior year had multiple unforeseen challenges. These challenges helped my superpowers to be exposed. The PAID factor helped me to implement my strategy and get various people involved in my plans. By embracing my superpower, I was prepared to face new challenges like go to college without knowing how I will pay for it. Because of my PAID superpower and the problem-solving skills I developed during my senior year, I was able to find a path to college on a full scholarship. I even graduated from college after the untimely death of my mother.

I learned a lot about myself and other people during these challenges. I believe it was my positive attitude and intense determination that led to my success. This superpower has been useful in both my professional and personal life. There have been times in my personal life where PAID has helped me to save family relationships and friendships. In the workplace, I have been able to use these skills to get the right teams together, to have positive collaborations and to develop the technology needed for successful programs. One thing in particular, you can't do everything on your own and don't be afraid to ask for help!

As we go through our daily lives there will be challenges even struggles but we must be able to rise up, stand up and sometimes make a shift if we are going to get to our desired goals. God wants us all to have success in our lives, your success might not be the same as my success but just know if you can keep a PAID something positive is bound to occur. Know your strength, don't be too proud to ask for help, and remember there are people in your life who want to see you succeed. Knowing oneself gives you the strength to persevere.

  Even though I would be the first in my family to go to a four-year college there were numerous challenges every day. I learned that challenges are just a part of life and can make you stronger. My motto of Dream, Believe, Achieve (DBA) has allowed me to do some incredible things and meet some incredible people. But I continue to find success by believing in God, having faith in the process and family by my side, I will get paid!

Antwan Brown

Antwan Brown is a Washington, DC native born on August 23rd, 1978. Growing up with his mother and brother in a single parent-single income household, Mr. Brown was forced to move throughout Prince George's County in search of affordable housing. Antwan graduated from Forestville High School where he played basketball, baseball, and football. Beyond sports, Mr. Brown was involved in Future Business Leaders of Tomorrow which gave high school students the opportunity tour organizations and government facilities and was teach students various business concepts.

Antwan was blessed with his first son in January 1996, just a year before he graduated Forestville High School in 1997. This only cemented his decision to continue his education at Livingstone College in Salisbury, NC. Even while attending Livingstone College, he balanced raising his son, being a part of the PTA at his son's elementary school, and duties as Vice President of the Livingstone College SGA, Student Activities Board, Phi Beta Lambda Business Fraternity. He graduated Livingstone College in May 2002 with his Bachelor of Science Degree in Computer Information Systems.

Mr. Brown decided to join the US Army as a Specialist where he was assigned to Fuel and Electrical Repair. He went on to lead countless field exercises and operated in South Korea as the driver and assistant to the Company Commander. Among his many tasks in Korea, Antwan Brown still found the time to be a part of and join Alpha Phi Alpha Fraternity, Inc before the end of his deployment. Mr. Brown was then relocated to Fort Bragg, NC where he noticed a gap between the newer younger soldiers and their sergeants. He began a rigorous mentor program for younger soldiers adapting to the military life, giving him a role as unofficial liaison. Mr. Brown was honorably discharged from the United States Army in 2005.

Once home Antwan's commitment to the youth and the community drove him to volunteer as an Extreme Teen at William Beanes Elementary school where he mentored a number of young men and helped a couple get into college. He continued to further his education by graduation from Webster University with a Master's in then earned his Master's in Business Leadership. His love for mentoring grew into a leadership role as Director of Residence Life at Wilberforce University, where he provided leadership, and oversight, to a community of over 500 students, and his support staff. Antwan was promoted to Assistant Dean of Continuing Education where he coordinated the planning, development, and implementation of the adult continuing education division.

Mr. Brown has returned home to focus on using his skills to help better his community. Antwan was elected President of the Birchwood Clearview Community Association, where he currently resides with his younger son and wife of 10 years. Antwan hopes to continue his mission to serve his community by being elected for the Democratic Central Committee for legislative district 26.

The Wolverine Effect

Welcome to my unleashing your superpower entry. It is a privilege and an honor to be able to be a part of this book and to share my superpower with you. When you finish this chapter, my hope for you is that you come away with the ability to follow your dreams, complete your goals, and gain motivation to get started and to keep going. I will tell you a few stories about my life to help you relate to the superhero within yourself. This book is just one of the ways that I am starting my journey of helping others figure out ways to accomplish the things that are needed to succeed.

I chose The Wolverine Effect for the title of this chapter because of the different characteristics, and abilities of the character. Don't know who Wolverine is? Well, Wolverine, a Marvel Comics character, is a mutant who has several superhuman characteristics that I am going to explore throughout this chapter. He is also a part of the X-Men. I believe in order to be a great superhero you should have several superpowers. Life brings you many challenges and having different ways to fight through them could only help you navigate through life better. Please take notes and write down what you have learned from this chapter.

At the end of each superpower I share with you a lesson I learned from the Wolverine Effect and how it has helped me navigate each moment of my life. I charge you to do the same thing. After reading all the stories in the book identify your superpower and write down a few lessons you learned from others. Let's get started. The first power that I identify within Wolverine is the ability to be indestructible.

Indestructible:

Definition: incapable of being destroyed, ruined or rendered ineffective (Webster)

Physically, human beings have the capability of being destroyed, ruined, and of course dying. You can attempt to gain strength or longevity by eating right and staying fit. What if you similar steps toward strengthening your mind and your mental ability? By doing that, you can create an area where you are potentially indestructible. Being incapable of letting the pains of the past destroy you, having the ability to not let people's words ruin you, and allowing the words of the naysayers to be ineffective to all your goals and plans are the aims for this first superpower.

Wolverine was born with old bones as his skeleton. Although they were old, they were still strong, and he had the ability to fight with the best of them. But they were not indestructible. When Wolverine was manipulated to go to the lab, he was altered to be used as a weapon and that's when he became indestructible. As individuals we have our own labs to enter which is quite different than what

Wolverine experienced. Our lab is life's circumstances. We may have to read, pray, or meditate to find a way to transform our mental skeleton in order to become the most indestructible person we can be in order to achieve our dreams.

As a young boy, I didn't realize that I had a learning disability. I just thought people in my school were much smarter, and I had to work harder to keep up. This made school very challenging and what didn't help was the fact that it was hard to identify children with a learning disability back then. Teachers sometimes lumped me with the "bad" kids, or "special needs" kids, and no one wanted to be labeled as either one. Another reason school was challenging was due to the number of schools I attended before graduating from the sixth grade. My family moved around a lot due to my mother being a single mom and for her to manage the constant rent increase she simply moved to another apartment so that she can stay within her budget. This ultimately led me to attending 11 different elementary schools, 2 junior high schools, and 3 high schools. Honestly, this didn't help teachers or the school system have a chance to help identity that one of their students has a learning disability. Somewhere along the way, I developed the mental indestructability. My classmates would tell me I was dumb. My teachers believed I was incapable of completing my assignments. The administrators didn't seem to care if I did well or not. During this struggle, I made a choice not to let my shortcomings stop me from moving forward to the next grade level. I didn't accept the label of a bad student, a bad son, or a bad person. My Wolverine Effect was learning how to be mentally indestructible. I chose to be a productive person in a community, an environment that didn't have much faith and didn't believe I would accomplish much at all.

The young boy in me had all the reasons in the world to give up and fail since that is what was expected of me and other young boys around me. But by building indestructible faith in myself I knew I could do anything I set my mind to and that's what helped me with my educational challenges. To this day those fears show up as I attempt new things (such as writing this chapter). Wolverine Effect Lesson on Being Indestructible: Remember the ability to be indestructible takes courage. You have to know you are still going to get hurt, have fears, and even possibly fail. Wolverine was physically indestructible. He was born with indestructible bones as a kid, but he didn't realize it until later in life. It wasn't until he was angry about the death of a man who he thought was his father when his claws appeared. His anger brought them out and the man he did kill with them was his real father. So he ran knowing that people would not understand what happened and would try to destroy him for his past sins and for what he had become. But as the definition explains, you are incapable of being destroyed, ruined or rendered ineffective. Apply that definition to your mental abilities so you can take this first superpower and move forward from all the things that are holding you back from becoming the person you want and need to be. You may need to pray, or meditate, but find your way of gaining that mental indestructibility. Remember, the challenges of your past can be hard, but moving forward no matter what helps you create your next superpower which is Super Strength.

Super Strength:

Definition: the capacity of an object or substance to withstand great force or pressure. (Webster)

Superheroes don't always have just one superpower. They have many superpowers that together make them superheroes. For example, Superman was able to fly, he had X-ray vision, laser beams for eyes, and super strength. So, let's talk about Wolverine's second superpower, super strength. At an early age, I realized that strength was both mental and physical. You must have the ability to look at problems head-on and deal with them as they come. The super-strength we are going to focus on in this part is the mental ability. You must use your strong mentality to make the right decision, form plans, and learn from your mistakes so that you can stick to your goals and move forward.

   At the age of 17, while a junior in high school, I found out that I was going to be a father. We all know how this happened, but there were circumstances that led to this. I made the choice not to go to the school that my mother wanted me to attend. At this point this was high school number two. It was about 3 years since we moved and I was liking the fact that I had friends, and teachers that I got to know and love. But when you get in trouble for just being around and hanging with the wrong group sometimes changes have to be made. A major group fight happened in my school because one neighborhood didn't like the other. Oh, and of course, a girl was involved. I held a hat for one of the kids from my neighborhood as he began to fight a young man from the other neighborhood. When it was all over the administration said I was involved simply because I was there. Rather than having an expulsion on my record my mother chose to withdraw me from school since we recently moved. Well, let's say I was not happy about this and decided once I got to the new school I was not going to attend. The new school had metal detectors, and police at the main entrance like something out of a movie. Living in the suburbs at this moment seems to have its perks, and I wanted back. But my mother was not having it, so I did what I thought was the next best thing, I skipped school and went over to the other side of town where all my friends were. Not to mention, the young lady I was talking to at the time was down for the meet-ups. I'll spare you the details just say boy meets girl, and girl gets pregnant after a few months of this routine. Now I have to get my mind ready to be a father. I ask myself tons of questions. Are you ready? Do you want kids? How would I support a kid? When will my mother kill me? I couldn't answer any of these questions and thank God my mother didn't kill me. But as a 17-year-old BOY, I decided school is not for me anymore, I'm going to get a job and provide for my new family. I was working for ROY ROGERS, a chicken company. I thought I was fairly good at working the front and back of the store and if I worked hard enough, I could become supervisor and then a manager. Boom, my kid will be taken care of. Who needs school, it was not making me any money to feed this mouth I had coming to the world? Mentally I was adjusting to what I thought was the correct way to provide the perfect outcome to raising a kid financially. Not knowing that being a father was not about the money, but much, much more. But the Wolverine in me would not let me fail at being the best father I could be as a 17-year-old BOY. In my mind I believed in order for my child to make it he has to have a man in his life that will do what it takes to be successful and help him succeed. I felt I didn't have that, and I didn't want that for my son. It was time to break the cycle. Thanks to some great administrators that came to my house to talk to me about a high school diploma vs a GED, and even the possibility of a bachelor's degree I decided to stay in school and complete my senior year. It was tough but knowing what I wanted for my son was something I didn't have for myself gave me the mental strength to move beyond my circumstances to finish high school and eventually move on to get a graduate degree. Wolverine Effect Lesson on being Mentally Strong: If you have read any of the comics, or seen any of the Wolverine movies you can see that his physical strength is undeniable. But as we look into our superhero more deeply his mental strength has to be noticed also. The ability to go through several different wars, fighting and dealing with the different losses he had over many years showed his mental fortitude. What we can learn from him is that we will go through many battles in life, but if we tap into the power of our mind to be brave and stay the course, we will be able to fight pass anything we struggle with here on this earth. The Wolverine in us will have the ability to grow and be a better soldier from all of the training we gain from our past experiences which will become our greatest strength.

Regenerate:

Definition: bring into renewed existence; generate again the third and final superpower we will be discussing will be Wolverine's ability to regenerate when he has been harmed. His ability to regenerate allows his to age very slowly which causes him to have a long life, and create lots of long lasting memories. Most people would look at this ability as a strength but for this book, I want you to think about this particular power as a weakness. Continue to read as I share with you what I believe could have been Wolverine's biggest weakness.

Just like Wolverine we have the ability to regenerate. In fact, non-injured tissues will regenerate over time. To stay with the theme of this chapter let's talk about our mind.

Everyday we have the ability to regenerate memories, both good and bad. Sometimes those bad memories can be very damaging to our present life. From a young boy I always thought that being a politician would be the perfect job for me. To me these politicians were helping people, talking on television, and attending major parties. Who wouldn't want to be a politician? In college, I became the Vice-President of our Student Government Association (SGA) my sophomore year. I also volunteered with various organizations on campus. A part of me really wanted to do what I can to pursue all kinds of leadership positions to help me become a politician, but my memories of not being a great student, having a learning disability, and people telling me what I could not do, kept me from pursuing that passion. Those memories would regenerate themselves in my head every time I had the option to move down that path. I allowed it to stop me and as life went on I did everything from working at fast food restaurants, coaching basketball, and I even became a dean at a university. However, that dream of wanting to be in a political office to serve people never left. Well, in 2010 I got my chance. I decided to run for a local seat in my hometown of Prince George's County MD. I was super excited. I was a young 30-year-old man trying to work for my community. I felt like I really had a chance to win, and because of this I was about to achieve my lifelong dream. But I guess the universe had different plans for me because I LOST the election. I didn't come in last so that was a big victory for me, but that lost stirred up all sorts of memories that supported the fact that I wasn't smart enough, to achieve this dream. The memories of the kid that couldn't write well, being left back in the second and fifth grades. The failures of letting my mother down because I had a kid while still in high school. Even the thoughts of what would my family think of me because I lost. The pain that came from this one event in my life stirred up years of negative events that happened in my past. What was I to do? How would I move forward?

As mentioned, the power to regenerate can be both good and bad. Those negative memories can be regenerated and can hold you back from achieving your goals, however you should know that the same power can be used to regenerate positive memories, thoughts and emotions. What helped me was a combination of all three powers. Having the mental indestructibility and strength allowed me to regenerate positive memories so I could start fresh and move forward. It took me several years to get the power and strength to run again, but in 2018 I did run. I was able to pull from all the lessons I learned my last experience and I got my victory. I was elected. WOW!!!

Learning to notice when your superhero is weak is very important. Wolverine Effect Lesson on Regeneration: There was only one thing that could stop Wolverine and that is the metal from his body created in a bullet form. This is exactly how our memories can be used to stop us. An event, thought, or emotion can cause certain memories to regenerate themselves in our mind and shoot down our dreams and accomplishments. To live the life you want, you have to be careful you are not giving your mind the bullets to shoot you. We have the power to do great things for our families, friends, and community if we just don't let our past get in the way. Every day we have to push forward and only look back as a reminder, not a deterrent. It took me 8 years to run for office again because I was afraid of failure. It wasn't until I faced fear head-on I was able to accomplish my dream.

Conclusion

When you unleash your superpower you are capable of doing whatever you put your mind to. Hopefully, these personal stories from my past can give you an indication of how the mind can work for good and evil. Wolverine had indestructible metal skeleton and skin that can regenerate to become perfect again. You have the same powers with your mind, so go out and develop the courage to conquer all the fears in your life. The mind is the strongest tool we as humans have, it's time to volunteer and go in the lab of life to unlock your superpower. Once you do you will be equipped with everything you need to achieve your purpose so you can help yourself and others. Who knows? You may even find a team of people with abilities like yourself and become your own version of X-MEN. Unleashing the Mind is the greatest superpower any of us can have. Unleashing my mind gave me the will to force myself to do amazing things even when people said it couldn't be done. What an amazing feeling!

Wolverine Effect LAST Lesson: YOU CAN DO ALL THINGS............!

Tawawn Lowe

Tawawn is the CEO of TL Enterprises, a woman-and minority owned multifaceted company based in Maryland that provide consulting, coaching/mentorship and training services to organizations and individuals; and the umbrella for TL Consultancy and the Women Walking in Their Own Shoes™ Movement.

Tawawn is an author, certified life coach and facilitator, Myers Briggs Indicator Type practitioner, speaker, 1 out of 250 certified vision board coaches/instructors nationwide, and creator of the Achieve Big Now Academy™.

She has blended her Bachelor of Science – Behavioral Studies degree, various certified credentials, and over 30+ years of professional experience to assist **organizations with communicating their vision and expanding and leveraging their talent management; and individuals with maximizing** their potential, transforming visions into goals, and to achieve results and success.

In October 2012, TLE expanded their mission and launched the Movement - Women **Walking in their Own Shoes** (WWITOS) ™. The Movement is a clarion call to action to women globally to say, "YES", giving themselves permission to become their best selves, create their best lives, and achieve success on their own terms (walking in their own shoes).

Tawawn goal is simple, to help others take charge of their destiny!

Untangled: Untying The Knots

Superpowers are Real. They are not just reserved for men and women wearing costumes hiding behind a mask.

When we think of superpowers it is always related to a fictional superhero character with superhuman powers or strengths who sacrifice themselves to fight crime and protect the innocent that plays out in a very imaginative story used to entertain.

The truth is we all have superpowers. Ordinary people like you and me are also gifted with superpowers. The distinction between fictional superheroes and us ordinary superheroes is our superpowers are not usually used for fighting crime and protecting the innocent. We don't fly, see through or leap tall buildings, turn into a green muscular humanoid with crazy strength, or have the ability to read people's thoughts, nor a magical lasso to make people tell the truth. Our superpowers are purposely bestowed to us. Uniquely designed to help us navigate our specific trials and tribulations, obstacles and roadblocks, and experiences that shape our reality. Our superpowers come to us in this gift called life. They help us to invoke purposeful transformation that amplifies our dreams and aspirations to be intentional about who we are, what we become, and what we achieve.

There are different formulaic ways in which fiction superheroes come into their powers. They are born with them, come into them by a certain age, through some freak scientific mishap, or through some major event or incident in which their powers are imparted unto them. However, us ordinary superheroes are born with our superpowers. They are innate. Our superpowers are hidden within us, in plain sight, and they only become awakened when we go through something that deeply changes our lives.

Fictional, or non-fictional, superheroes powers can only be unleashed when they are embraced and cultivated. I know my superpowers are real.

My superpower was awakened at a young age. It was the summer of 1976, I was 11 years old, transitioning to a new neighborhood, and from elementary school into junior high school. This was a very significant time in my life. It was a new beginning. And right in the midst of my new beginning, my father died. Losing my father had affected me intensely on so many levels. It was not because I would miss his presence, or more like the lack of his presence in my life.

My relationship with my father was short. We had just reconnected before he passed away. So, he had come and gone again, but this time it was permanent. His death left me angry, but not for him, but for all the questions I had for him that would now go unanswered. I didn't know how, or what to feel about his death, about him, us, or our relationship. This was my first major loss. I knew I was sad, but I didn't quite know why. I had a lot of mixed feelings, but I didn't know how to express what those feelings were. I later learned that what I was experiencing was grief; and that grief has a way of entangling your feelings. Grieving was a process. To help me understand my grief, my mom took me to a child therapist, and it was through that experience where my first superpower was awakened.

Going to therapy at a young age had a profound effect on my life. Through my sessions, I learned the difference between feelings and thoughts, and that people often confused the difference between their emotions with thoughts, that emotions dictate their behavior, and how to ask probing questions. I remember walking into one of my sessions, matter-of-factly announcing to the therapist this will be my last day coming. Of course, the therapist asked why, and my response was I understand. Her next question was, 'What do you understand'? Now I can remember the conversation like it was yesterday, because it was on that day that I decided I wanted to be a child therapist. When she met with my mother after our session, as she always did, I could tell she was shocked by the events and conversation. I heard her tell my mother, "She is very perceptive".

In her conversation with my mother she recapped what we discussed. She told my mother of my announcement of that day being my last session, and my reasons why…….. "she believes that she now knows the root of her sadness surrounding her father's death. She never felt loved or wanted by her father. And those feelings and thoughts were the reason she was angry and being mean to people. Now that she knows her feelings is the cause of her anger. There is no need to be angry anymore. She said it was her father's loss because he waited forever to be in her life. And that she knew you loved her, and that was all that mattered, and that nothing could be done now because he was dead." She explained that in each of our sessions she always asked me the same two questions. What you are thinking, and how does that make you feel. That last session was the first time I ever responded, "I no longer cared or have any questions to why my father didn't love me". She proceeded to tell my mother that she had explored my response by asking "How do you know your father didn't love you?" And she reiterated my response, "because he never told me he did nor did he show it."

Needless to say, that was not my last session. She wanted to make sure I had some closure. I don't remember how many more sessions I had. I just remember trying to learn and understand everything she did. I had become consumed with wanting to be a therapist. I wanted to be like her. I wanted to know what made people tick. . It was through my sessions where my superpower was awakened. I had learned how to differentiate the difference between feelings and thoughts, to pay attention to patterns, to watch people behaviors to understand what they were feeling. Feelings were temporary, how to be perceptive and recognize when people were tangled, how to ask probing questions to get to the root of the knots; and that closure, time and patience were important to untying knots.

My highly innate intuitive superpower was first manifested when I untied the knots of how I felt about my father, our relationship, and his death. I was a dangerous child with a great superpower that was not effectively cultivated. My friends really didn't understand me, but I understood them, and adults started saying I had been here before. I was before my time. All my conversations lead to two questions - "how does that make you feel, and what do you think about that'? That was my open door to diagnose people entanglements, share my opinions, and a way of protecting or saving them with my unsolicited fixes.

As you know, with every superhero, there is a weakness that puts them in danger. It was in the last quarter of my seventh-grade year when a seed of self-limitation and underestimation was planted in my life vision. We had been given an aptitude test, and based on my low scoring, my teacher told me that my career opportunities were limited to the food service industry. She was specifically in telling me that I would never be anything beyond a cafeteria worker. At a time when I was being told I could become anything I put my mind to. I was being told my career aspirations should be no more than one of those cranky and mean women who served our lunch every day.

Once again, my life had become entangled, but this time I thought I knew how to protect and save myself. I knew I didn't feel good about what I was told, but my thoughts about my current reality were logical. I had asked myself all the right questions. And the outcome was that I had taken the test, so the results couldn't possibly be wrong. I accepted that this was just my life, and I would have to make the best of the hand I was dealt. I didn't not realize at 11 years old that I had the power to create my own destiny. I trusted my teacher, and those results. I later learned (at the age of 40) that I had scored high in humanities, and that my math scores were extremely low. As a child, I didn't understand that life and death are in the power of the tongue, and that teacher's words became my mantra, and would turn into a self-fulfilling prophecy. It was my kryptonite. Now my kryptonite was not some fictional crystalline material originating from some fictional place. My kryptonite was real. It was my self-limiting beliefs on what I could or could not achieve.

My first experience with my self-limiting beliefs did not become visible until I graduated from high school, and all my plans started to become tangled. There were so many disappointments, failures and missteps. As I tried to process myself through my feelings and thoughts, that seventh-grade teacher's words started to harvest. I could not figure out how to untangle the knot – it had caused great mental anguish while reducing my ability to absorb energy from my superpower.

By the time I reached my twenties, like some of the fictional superheroes, I started to hold back my original superpower for that one particular area of my life, and eventually I became crippled by my self-doubt to the point I didn't believe my life had purpose.

I learned to be numb about my potential. I put on a mask to hide my identity, and allowed my representative to take charge of that sensitive area of my life. I continued to use my superpowers in all the other areas of my life, to protect my insecurities and feelings of inadequacy while my new superpower allowed me to hide behind my fear and not confront my self-limiting beliefs. I had to figure out how I could confront my beliefs without the turmoil of the pain. Until I figured that out, I wandered through life with no vision or purpose for over fifteen years. I just took life as it was, a slow death. I was unfulfilled, unhappy and mad because I could almost figure out everything, but this...For more than that 5843.88 plus odd days, I had been able to think clearly without clouded judgment. I provided reasonable advice to help others. I allowed my addiction to help others cause me to believe if I walked in other shoes it would make me better. The problem was I couldn't walk in someone else's shoes, I needed to walk in my own shoes. In order to untie the years of knots I entangled, I had to start operating in my personal power.

God is funny. He has a way of getting your attention. I remember one day I got so frustrated and threw away my Coach tennis shoes because I couldn't untangle the knots. I kept looking at the shoestrings trying to figure out how did they get so entangled. Life is a lot like shoestrings. It can be pulled and stretched in different directions, get stained, become untied and unraveled. You can find yourself entangled into different types of knots that restrict your emotional, mental, physical and spiritual movement. Sometimes the shoestrings of life get so tangled they can just pop. That is what happened to me over all those years of avoiding my limiting beliefs.

The best way to untie a shoestring knot is to examine how it is tied. You have to be patient, and then little by little, you can meticulously pick apart the knot, slowly loosen it, and pass one end through the loops one by one. Untying the knots of your life also requires a mass conscious that stems a self-assessment, a deep look at yourself, answering the questions of how did get here, what started the knots, fortitude and the space for grace and forgiveness, and give careful attention to those areas that need to be loosed so can become the best version of yourself that you always envisioned. You have to be willing to relinquish your mask, expose your vulnerability, allow your weakness to break you, and learn how to grow stronger through the weakness. Life is choice driven, and I finally came to the realization that I had the power to change the trajectory of my life. I had forgotten that my superpowers were created especially for me, and it is hard to master and harness your superpowers when you have given up or giving away your personal power. I stopped mentally blocking people and situations and allowed myself to feel again. I used my degree in behavior science, minor in psychology and faith to change me from the inside out. After 2 years of blood, sweat and tears, I unleashed my superpower to save me. The process was not easy. Fighting against my kryptonite was emotionally and mentally draining. I slipped. I cried, called on Jesus to help me, but most importantly I never gave up.

There were seven critical principles I used help restore my belief system about myself, and turn my weaknesses into strengths:

1. Accept, Believe and Know 2. Exposed the Hidden Me 3. Started A New Journey 4. Understood the Power of Words 5. Adjusted my Attitude 6. Developed Faith Without Limits 7. Became My Own Cheerleader

Accept, believe and know was the starting point of my fight against my self-limiting beliefs. Adjusting my attitude concerning how I viewed, felt and thought about myself was vital. I had to accept that I wasn't what I believed, and that I was created on purpose with a purpose. I had to believe the new narrative I was telling myself no matter the disappointments and failures. I know what I accepted and believed was fact. This required a lot of face-to-face mirror time. Me talking to myself to reprogram my subconscious mind.

Exposing the hidden me was the hardest process. It was easy to say I was more than a conqueror, I was created on purpose, and I was not my experience. But taking off that mask, and peeling back those layers took inner energy and strengthen that I didn't know existed. I had to go to the cemetery in my mind and heart to close those unfilled graves that served as gaping wounds to my soul. Self-forgiveness played a big role at this stage. It was hard to stop punishing myself for my bad choices. Every day when I did my mirror talk, I apologized to myself, told myself I was sorry, and that I forgave me. At first, I didn't believe, but I kept saying it until I felt it. Once I started feeling it, I was believing. I knew I had not been living the life I wanted, so for the first time in life, I took responsibility for my happiness, joy, peace, and success. Starting a new journey was my next step after accepting, believing, knowing, taking off the mask, and forgiving myself. I realized I had no vision or goals for my life. I was driven to discover my purpose, have a vision for my life, and activate my goal positioning system that would guide me towards my purpose.

Understanding that life and death are in the power of my own tongue was key. For it was words that started and shaped my limited beliefs about myself. I had to learn that words had energy. The ability not only to hinder, but heal, and that I had to watch what I said to myself, and what I allowed people to speak into my life.

Attitude adjustment was about understanding perspective is everything, and my superpower had a direct tie into my perspective. My feelings and thoughts were all based on my perspective. That is why what I accepted, believed and knew about my truth was crucial. Faith without limits was just trusting that God loved me, he created me on purpose, and had a purpose for my life. My superpower was leading to my healing could only come through Him. I had to learn to be my own cheerleader. When you are down, or need that motivation, you can't always depend on others to give you, what they often don't have for themselves. I learned to let my why be my motivator, and to tell myself you go girl, we got this. These seven principles have become the foundation of my personal and spiritual growth and development. I keep my goal to be my best self, and create my best life in front of me daily.

Through each of these principles I always asked myself two important questions - "How does that make you feel and what do you think about that?" I pay attention to my patterns and ask those probing questions. My innate intuitive superpower has been properly cultivated and it plays a crucial role in how I live my life. My superpower has untangled me through the devastation of divorce, not being able to have children, having my adoptive child removed from my arms after raising her for 6 months, and other major life issues.

    My innate intuitive superpower has grown, made room for my gifts and talents, and it is still protecting me, helping me to transform into my best self, and create my best life.

    Superpowers are real!

Lisa Dove Washington

After tapping into her gifts and going after her dreams, Lisa Dove Washington has become a Media Entrepreneur whose services are in demand for her highly-recognized skills in social media marketing, event coverage, interviewing, and much more. Since the age of 12, Lisa has used her gift of gab to accomplish many things, including becoming the advice columnist for Dear Asil (Lisa spelled backwards). After graduating from high school, she attended Spelman College in Atlanta to major in English with a minor in Communications.

Lisa is the publisher of her global online magazine, *Dove Style Magazine*, which she launched in 2012 following her job as a contributing writer for *Celebrity Charity Magazine* out of California. She is sought after for her public relations skills and has had the opportunity to interview a variety of celebrities, such as Stacy Lattisaw Jackson, Donald

Lawrence, Tanya Blount, and Reverend Joseph Lowery to name a few, as well as doing features on local talent, foundations, and businesses from all over the country.

Lisa's list of accomplishments includes co-authoring two publications, *The Global Red Circle: Standing in Truth, Unleashing Our Most Powerful Selves* by Kim Andrews and *Artificial Beaute: The True Beaute Beneath the Surface – A Woman's Anthology* by Bonita Parker and releasing her first novel, *The Power of Shut Up*. Also, she edited a book from the extensive For Dummies series titled *Bowling for Dummies* written by A.J. Forrest and Lisa Iannucci. Touching on her acting abilities, Lisa was cast in several web series and the movie *C.E.O. (Criminal Enterprise Organization)* produced by Antwon Temoney.

Sought after to promote events via social media and provide event promotions and publicity, Lisa is putting her God-given gifts to work, and she is just getting started. Currently, Lisa is the co-host of the Girls Gabbin' Radio Show that airs every Sunday at 7:00 pm (EST) on WINDC Radio powered by GoWin Media. Her goal is to empower, enlighten, and inspire others to shine while living their dreams.

Lisa serves as a committee member of the Ebenezer Institute at Ebenezer A.M.E. United Methodist Church in Fort Washington, Maryland. The Ebenezer Institute was created to give the community options to enhance their education and skills. Lisa also serves on the Advisory Board for the STEM program at her former high school, H.D. Woodson High School, and is an active member and mentor of the "I Love Me" mentoring program founded by Ms. Darcel Collins in Maryland. The "I Love Me" program assists young women with educational, social, emotional, and professional enlightenment with an emphasis on the power of the mind, and Lisa feels blessed to be a part of the organization.

A native of Washington DC, Lisa is a devoted wife and the proud mother of two.

Contact Info:
Website: www.lisadovewashington.com
Email: Mrsldwashington@gmail.com
Facebook - Lisa Dove Washington
Instagram -@lisadovewashington
Twitter- @LWashingtonCCM

Peace Beyond the Pain

Having a Superpower does not mean that you are always great at something, nor does it mean that you like it. It does mean that you have accepted something that challenged you and made you better. I truly believe that I have always had a special "gift", but it wasn't until I got a little older, maybe around my early teens that I started to notice a pattern of behavior that would later on lead me to what I now consider my Superpower. I would soon discover that one of the hardest things I have ever had to do would be the very thing that would bless me in so many ways. That Superpower was Forgiveness! On the surface Forgiveness seems like a great thing, right? What a blessing to be able to forgive someone else, right? BUT, forgiveness can also be the most difficult thing you will ever have to do. Realizing that I had this "gift" actually proved to be a very scary thing for me. I would think to myself, "What is so great about forgiving someone who did something to hurt me?" You want someone who hurt you or did something to you to hurt the way you did for the wrongdoing. You want them to feel your pain when they are inconsiderate and thoughtless. I was mad that forgiveness came so easy, but it was mine and I had to own it. But life brings you disappointment and hurt until the day you die and not being able to forgive can destroy every opportunity you will have to LIVE and live in PEACE! Forgiveness always seemed to be something you always gave to another person who caused you pain, hurt your feelings or mis-treated you in some way. Along my journey of discovering my superpower, what I thought about Forgiveness would turn out to be the very opposite. It would be life-changing to say the least but the blessings that came with the understanding and acceptance were everything. As a young child, around the age of 11, I was violated by a neighbor during a visit to a friend's home. Something that I didn't deserve, nor did I expect it, but, in an instant this was part of my journey, my reality. To be violated as a child can be absolutely devastating and I am sure most would feel UNFORGIVEABLE! To be honest, I didn't even know the impact that it would have on my life until I got older. Because I was just a child and I didn't quite understand what to do with those feelings. I did nothing for years. When I even started to fully acknowledge what had happened, I was already at a place in my life where I understood what my Superpower was - Forgiveness. My Superpower was fully developed by the time I began dealing with this incident in my life. I believe I confronted/acknowledged (pick one) the violation at that time because I could handle it emotionally. I never focused on the anger and hurt but more so focused on protecting others and not letting it affect my future. At such a young age, that is a huge burden to bear, but God knows you before you know yourself and my Superpower allowed me to not let this moment in time hinder me from moving forward in life. But this would not be the first hurt that required my Superpower. Now we all fall in love, most times, over and over again right? And along with falling in love comes heartache! It's almost a guarantee that your heart will break at least once. Well, I have definitely had my share of heartaches and heartbreaks over the years and I will venture to say that relationships are sometimes the hardest to forgive because you have willingly fallen in love with someone who start to trust and once you put all your trust in to that person, it's inevitable. You almost forget that they are human too and will make many mistakes. It's a fact of life. But, it is how you handle those disappointments and hurts that helps get you through it. Being deceived and cheated on by a love is a painful thing. You know that feeling of flying high on love feeling that the man or woman you love with everything in you would never do anything to hurt you, only to find out that they have cheated on you or done something to you that caused you pain?

    Horrible feeling, right? Absolutely! It's a feeling that some people never get over. It destroys lives sometimes permanently, but it doesn't have too. I was a teenager lost in love. Nothing felt better and life was great. And then I found out something that devastated me. My boyfriend was cheating on me. I hadn't been receiving calls from him lately and wanted to know what was going on. We didn't live close to each other nor did we go to the same school. My phone calls were going unanswered and I couldn't take it anymore so who do I call? I called his best friend because if anybody knew what was going on, it would be him. So we talk and I ask 1000 questions about why he may not be calling me back. He kept assuring me that there was nothing going on as far as he knew and that he was just busy after school most days. That is when we came up with a plan to find out and hopefully make me feel better about not hearing from him. Of course, he wanted to reassure me that there was no funny business going on. Remember back in the day when having conference calls with your friends on the phone was so much fun? Well, that's what we decided to do, but the difference was that he was going to call him with me on the phone and ask him questions to re-assure me that he was just really busy and there was nothing crazy going on. Sounded like a plan to me so that's just what we did. I stayed silent on the phone as my boyfriend's best friend talked with him asking questions here and there about what he was up to and how his classes were going, etc. And then something happened that was unexpected. My boyfriend, who had no idea that I was on the phone, started to share with his best friend about some girl that he was talking to and how he gave her a chain that I had recently given him to wear. WHAT the %#%$@$! I was devastated. I couldn't believe what I was hearing. My worst fear was now my reality. Believe it or not, blame it on the shock, lol, I stayed quiet on the phone so that I didn't expose his best friend because he was also my friend and he had done a great favor (if that's what you want to call it) for me. The hurt that I was feeling at that moment was indescribable. I cried all day and all night for days, but after that, I hated him. (You know teenage love can be so dramatic). I did call my boyfriend eventually and yes, we broke up after that. And oh yeah, I definitely got my chain back, think I didn't? But I never told him how I found out. Ironically enough, I ran into him a little while later and was able to say hello with a smile on my face with not one bit of anger. I had already forgiven him because the weight was too heavy to bear. You would have thought that I would want to cuss him out and smack him up and down the street but the thought never crossed my mind. Like I said, the pain of disappointment, betrayal never lasts forever unless you let it. I allowed the betrayal to keep me from trusting people. It was hard for me to believe what people said. That's the thing that I learned about having a Superpower. It doesn't always kick in. Sometimes you have to learn what it takes to bring it to the surface. Maybe I hadn't completely forgiven him for hurting me so it simply followed me. While he had moved on, maybe I was still holding on to a bad memory. That is what not forgiving will do, which meant there was still work to be done. I personally believe that you are not always a pro at your superpower and sometimes you are not even the best at it. Knowing your superpower though will continue to remind you to step up to the plate when you fall short. Heartbreak from a love is a real hard challenge. But believe it or not, one of the biggest hurts and disappointments that I have ever had to deal with has come from those who were closest to me. You grow up thinking that the people who surround you every day or those who are your blood relatives would never hurt or betray you, but as you live, you learn! You start to realize that hurt comes in all shapes and sizes and it can come from anyone - friends and family included. I would learn that being lied to, cheated on, mis-treated or treated less than would come from the very people that you lovingly called "Family". Unfortunately it all happens to us at different times and phases of our lives. The past few years of my life I have truly been challenged. I have experienced hurt in ways that I never expected. The pain was so great that Forgiveness was the last thing on my mind. Some of you can relate and some are still working on forgiveness. Anyone who knows me, knows I am all about family! My family has always been a huge part of my life and I have always done everything I can to keep family close and to support them in any way. I believed that no matter who treats you wrong, leaves you out, talks about you behind you back, or even lies and betrays you, it wouldn't be your family. Not my family anyway. My family had gathered together to celebrate my late Grandmother's 100th birthday and no one invited me to the celebration. I felt like a moment in life had been stolen from me. Not just a moment to celebrate my grandmother but a moment to be with my family. I felt like I was punched in the gut by a professional fighter twice my size. And he was wearing brass knuckles when he hit me. I didn't think I would ever heal from this. I couldn't believe it. The anger that came over me once it was discovered what went down was a feeling that I had not felt since that cheating boyfriend incident. How could Family do something like that to another member of their family? Being left out of something special was hurtful. And that wasn't even the worst part. The worst part was that no one seemed to feel bad about it. No one tried to understand how the decision to exclude me would hurt deeply and no one ever reached out to say I AM SORRY! It was the most unexpected act from the most unexpected culprits. I knew at that moment, that among other things, this was something that I would never forgive. How would you feel to realize that your family felt that you were that insignificant to an event that the rest of the family felt was a big deal? Exactly! This changed my whole concept of how what I believed family was about and what lines family would cross. I know that people are people, but what you expect from your family is usually a lot more than you expect from a stranger.

Through this situation, I learned some valuable lessons. The first lesson was that getting over something like this was extremely hard. I felt like I was treated as a non-factor to the very people that I thought valued my feelings. Deep down I knew I had to forgive them, but the truth was I didn't want to. I didn't feel that they deserve forgiveness. They didn't even care about the pain they caused, why should I forgive them? I had to learn for the first time how to forgive without ever receiving an apology or even acknowledgement of wrongdoing. I can honestly say that I prayed immensely about what to do because everything in me was pushing to NOT forgive. I had to make some tough decisions from this incident and forgiveness was going to have to be first. The inner battle was real, but then I remembered that I can't deny my Superpower. I can't deny the fact that I know the best thing for me is to forgive them. I had some tough decisions to make after this because I never want to feel that pain again. I did get to a place where I could forgive but I also made a promise to myself. See, I do believe that no one, and I mean no one has the right to intentionally hurt or mis-treat you. The second lesson is how I relate to people who I have forgiven moving forward. I had to learn what I will tolerate. I decided that forgiveness was absolutely necessary, but I had to protect my peace. I chose to walk away from these family members. I now define what "family" means to me and I am at peace more than I have ever been. With every superpower comes a responsibility and that is where the real you show up. Now I never said that having my superpower of forgiveness was easy, nor wanted, but I do know that it was given to ME. It was my responsibility to understand it, embrace it and learn from it as I exercise it. The things I learned as I discovered my Superpower of Forgiveness: 1. Forgiveness is Necessary 2.

Forgiveness brings Peace 3. Forgiveness brings Freedom 4. Forgiveness is for you, not them 5. Forgiveness provided me with focus 6. Lack of forgiveness will hold you prisoner 7. The more I forgive, the easier it becomes to do 8. Forgiveness can hurt for a while but never forever 9. Forgiveness is learning to accept the apology you might never receive 10. Forgiveness can be the most difficult thing to do, but also the most rewarding

     I spent a lot of time fighting my superpower because I thought I was giving those who hurt me a pass. I even thought I was keeping them from suffering the consequences of hurting me. But, when I was unforgiving, I was only hindering and blocking my own peace of mind. To forgive someone for doing something to you frees you from the pain they caused. You can now move beyond that pain and grow as a person. I learned that I can't grow in unforgiveness. Forgiving others is a form of letting go and moving on! I struggled tremendously at first - lots of tears, anger, and prayer. It was a constant struggle and challenge. Forgiving others seemed to come easy. The hard part was that I didn't want to do it. When you start to realize that the things that hurt you are lessons that will help you to grow, it lessens the struggle or the fight to defy your superpower. Because of the peace I gained from my discoveries, I was inspired to share what I have learned with others. What I found to be my "Kryptonite", or my weaknesses in discovering my Superpower of Forgiveness was my anger, my emotions, my desire to "payback." I can admit it now. I wanted revenge. I wanted to treat them like they treated me. And these feelings kept me from moving forward in my superpower. What will I do to prepare myself for the moments when my Superpower will be challenged? When I find myself getting caught up in my "Kryptonite"? How do I keep from holding back on doing what was needed and what was right? I stopped listening to my emotions and I listen to God instead. I ask God for guidance and strength to make the right decisions. Emotions can play a big part in distracting you from doing what's right, so I try to make sure that I am not acting through my emotions. This can be very challenging and to be truly transparent, without thought sometimes, I move when I am sad, angry or hurt and then afterwards, I regret the move. Another powerful lesson that I learned in discovering my Superpower is learning the Power Of Shut Up. When I acted in my emotions, I usually said something that I didn't mean. Once it is said, I couldn't take it back. Learning to stop and listen to God before I act OR speak has been a second superpower that I explore in depth in my latest book properly entitled The Power Of Shut Up. (You may want to put the information here on how to get the book...or not) Discovering my Superpower of Forgiveness has ultimately brought me Peace beyond the Pain!

Quashon Davis

Quashon Davis is a bestselling author who is best known for his trilogy: Masquerade, The Dirty Circle, and Suspect Behavior. He was awarded with the book of the year award in 2006 from the prestigious Imani Book club, and the author to look out for in 2017 by the New York Times.

After writing his first novel at the age of fourteen, Quashon knew he was destined to share his unique style and creativity with the world. A jack of all trades, he always comes back to his writing, which always relaxes him. He's been a journalist, sports analyst, on air host, event host, and even a stand-up comedian, but his writing is his true passion. His ability to compose thought provoking stories earned him a cult following in the New York/New Jersey metro area. He currently hosts a podcast and his successful 'female nightmares' series has been picked up by a film director. Despite all of this, Quashon still finds time to watch movies and play video games.

You're Down, Now Get Up!

Have you ever been down? I mean really down? You ever struggle to get out the bed in the morning not because you didn't feel like seeing anyone, but because you didn't want anyone to see you? In our lifetime we end up mentally hurt hundreds of times, but I'm willing to bet you can remember the two or three worse times. For some of you, when you're hurt, you're able to shrug it off and keep going on with your life. That's a great strength to have, believe me. For many of us, when we're hurt or down, we fall into a dark place that we can't seem to climb out of. Think of it as if you're a car: you need oil for the car to run; as that oil gets dirty it affects the performance of the car. As you go through difficult times, that 'oil' gets dirty. Your mind and body (the car) begins to run poorly. If you don't address the things that are bothering you, you can never get better. Your 'car' will always run poorly. Eventually that car breaks down. While we all go through periods of stress and disappointment, some of us change our oil: addressing the issues that are affecting us negatively and moving on from them before they become an issue that brings us down. Unfortunately, many people never change their oil. They're mind state becomes foggy and slowly deteriorates.

Being able to heal and recover is a superpower that a lot of people don't have. It has nothing to do with being sensitive either. I was always a happy go-lucky guy. I was the one that everyone came to when they needed a good laugh. I never knew what depression even was. By the age of twenty-five, I'd done stand-up comedy, played ball in the toughest spots in the city, and even appeared in a movie. I was always on the move. I had some minor challenges, but nothing ever brought my mood down (I changed my oil often). By the age of 27, I thought I was ready to have a family. I got married, bought a house, and finally slowed down. I thought it was the natural progression of things. I was ready to move on to the next happy chapter of my life. It was 2001, I was still thin and athletic, and had an almost permanent smile on my face.

By 2004, I weighed 320 pounds. I was in a marriage that was void of respect, honesty, trust, and money. I came home everyday and forced myself to go into the house after sitting in the driveway for at least an hour. I lived off credit cards and avoided my family and friends. All I thought about was dying. Every night I would sit on the porch for hours, until the sun came up. Every night, I would sit there in tears trying to understand how I ended up in that position. My wife was openly cheating. I was sleeping on the couch, and trying to survive on 35 dollars a month spending money. I remember the night on the porch that I decided to end it all.

How did I get there? I allowed it to happen. I allowed my heart to fill with pain and hurt until it couldn't take anymore. Getting out of bed became more and more difficult. The funny thing about depression is that it's like dog mess: you never see it in front of you, and then BOOM, you step right in it (and you can't get it off). Hitting rock bottom is a feeling that a lot of people never recover from. Lucky for me, I discovered that I had a superpower deep in me - **the ability to quickly recover and heal.** I just didn't know it yet.

I decided to end it all on a Monday. I always hated Monday's so it just made sense. Besides, my friends are trifling. If my funeral service was during the week, I knew they wouldn't show up. The things you think about when you're depressed. I was 320 pounds; I knew that meant extra pallbearers. The old people would be sitting there gossiping about me while eating my mothers' famous macaroni salad. Man, I was really going through it.

I went from getting down once in a while about my situation to being depressed all the time. I never changed my oil, and it showed. Anytime I sat still for longer than a minute, I could feel tears forming in my eyes. The freight train called life had run me over, and it left me a broken damaged mess. Instead of trying to address my issues and heal from them, I allowed them to grow inside of me, like a virus. That untreated virus ravaged my system. I felt like there was no coming back from it. The only way out was death.

The night before that Monday I spent the night on the porch thinking. As much as I despised my wife, part of my depression stemmed from the fact that I wasn't providing for the household the way I was supposed to. As a man, your job is to make sure that your wife wants for nothing, and I wasn't doing that. She let me know this every chance she got. I had a pretty good job: I was teaching at a charter school in New Jersey. I went from making about 32 grand at the Port Authority to banking 62K at a private charter school. The principal was a 'friend' of a couple of my family members. Even though I didn't have whatever was officially needed to teach, they had me teaching. Well, when the state came in and started looking around, the principal covered his ass by firing me and accusing me of everything from stealing textbooks to teaching without credentials. He's the one that made me teach without credentials! This was after we had purchased a home, so it got difficult fast. After messing around with unemployment for a few months, I had to take a security job making 15 bucks an hour. Man, we went downhill fast!

    I got deep in debt so fast I didn't even realize what was going on! With a twenty four hundred dollar mortgage payment, and a three hundred fifty dollar car note, bringing home 2 grand a month wasn't good. By the time the smoke cleared every month I didn't have anything. I thought I was still good though. I was still the jokester barbecuing for my friends every weekend. The bills were piling up and late fees were everywhere. One day I was in the basement playing video games and a tear rolled down my cheek. I looked around confused as more and more tears made their way down my face. That's when it hit me: I was depressed. I had heard about depression, but I didn't really believe in it. I always thought people used the term as an excuse to mope around. I was very wrong. I cut everyone off and didn't even realize it. I was sad all the time. It felt like it happened overnight, but I know it didn't. Losing the job, trying to find another one, struggling with bills, late fees- they all played a part in the buildup leading to depression. I still hadn't changed my oil. My wife and I barely spoke, unless she was going off about something. I was stuck in this situation for what I thought would be the rest of the life.

If you've ever read a comic book, you know how most heroes come to be. Of course some are born with powers, but the most compelling stories are the ones where the hero discovers his special abilities. That night on the porch was the equivalent of that moment. I really thought about all of the deep issues I had. I thought about all the instances where I felt emasculated and embarrassed. I thought about when my wife got her master's degree: how smug and cold she was toward me at her graduation. She was looking down on me. It was something I had never noticed before, but it was really bothering me. I thought about how much I loved my mother. She is the ultimate inspiration. Honestly, thinking about her made me realize I had a superpower!

When I was born, my mom was young. She didn't collect child support, and he didn't do a damn thing for me. Her guidance counselor infamously told her to take up a trade. When my brother was born, we were on welfare. We ate fish sticks five nights a week! My mom easily could've quit. She had been knocked down several times, hit rock bottom more than once. That woman still put herself through college and law school, raising two boys with no help. She, my mom, is a judge now. How could I sit on that porch and give up, when the person I looked up to the most would never tap out under any circumstances?

I realized my mom had **the power to heal and recover quickly.** She had been knocked down countless times, but she never gave up on herself. She got down sometimes but she never stayed there. I watched my mom lose jobs, struggle with money, catch the bus, and even go without eating so we could eat. I never saw her get down on herself. To this day, I've never seen her cry! I've never seen her blame anyone. She just keeps pushing forward.

Did I have that same superpower?

If I did, why was I down and out for so long?

Was it because half of me was concocted from him, a known quitter? Maybe I had it…but I needed to unleash it! I had so many things left to accomplish. The night on the porch meant to reminisce before ending it all turned into a long evening, listing things I still had to do.

I unleashed my superpower.

That next day I enrolled at a University. I started out taking three classes. I joined the gym, and quickly came down fifty pounds. I wrote and published a novel. I packed my stuff and moved out. On my way out the door she told me that she saw other men because I wasn't a real man. I didn't handle my business like a real man would. She threw one final jab at me: a last attempt to send me back to that dark place, but I wouldn't fall. I vowed to never let myself get down like that again. **Life is hard, real hard, and I've had tough times since then, but I quickly recover, heal and move forward. That's my superpower**. There's always going to be things in life that will bring you down, give you heartache, even physically affect you. The way you deal with these things will determine everything from your future to your health. Emotional stress that lingers for weeks or months can weaken the immune system and cause high blood pressure, anxiety, disease, depression, even heart disease.

Recovery is more than just the process of healing from an injury or illness. Think of a kid that breaks his arm falling off a swing. How does it heal? The doctor puts it in a cast and the kid doesn't use it for a couple of months. Now think of when your heart is hurt by something and apply that method to it. Someone or something has hurt you, so your first step is acknowledging that you're hurt. Admitting what has occurred is the equivalent of the doctor putting the broken arm in a cast. Why? Because the same way the broken arm won't heal without a cast, you won't heal until you can admit you have something you need to heal from. Then you can put your cast on and start healing.

    I know a guy who lost his Dad when he was 10 years old. He's been in a depression about it his entire life. He's gone on to have a family of his own and still goes to weekly therapy to deal with the pain of losing his father. He's 41 years old. He just can't seem to get over it.

    A wise woman once told me *'you can't tell someone how to feel.'* That is absolutely true. However, going decades and never getting over a trauma is a tough one. You can't live out your future to the fullest if you're dealing with things from your past. After admitting that you're hurt, the healing can begin. Now you put that broken limb in a cast. You do that by facing what hurt you head on. Did it kill you? Why did it do this much damage to your psyche? Once you can answer that, moving forward becomes easier. For me, I was depressed and severely overweight. My daily intake consisted of 2 McDonalds Chicken Biscuits in the morning, chased with a big bowl of Frosted Flakes. For lunch I had two value meals from one of the fast food chains, and dinner was either a whole pizza, or two- dozen wings and some cheese bread. In between all that, I had plenty of snacks. I allowed myself to feel emasculated by my situation and my mate, and after falling into a deep state of depression; I ate myself into a ridiculous state. So what did this superpower of healing and recovery allow me to do? I started by getting to the root of my issues. I didn't feel like I was being the man I needed to be. I had lost my job, and we were struggling. My wife was verbally abusive, constantly reminding me of how 'real men' don't find themselves in that type of situation. 'Real men' was the root of my issue. I never felt like I was the prototypical man's man. I didn't have any kids, which was a big deal to me. Men have kids, men raise sons (and daughters). That's what a real man is supposed to do, and I wasn't doing that. I wasn't good with my hands either. I'm useless at Home Depot. I used to sit and play video games while she put tables together from IKEA. She handled all the household bills and tax stuff. I paid, but it was just me giving her money every month. When I thought about it, I felt more like the wife. I allowed this. I allowed myself to feel inferior. I didn't have a college education, she did. I was living with my mother when we met; she was living on her own. I didn't know how to cook, clean, pay bills, or live independently. Once I realized all the reasons why I was really depressed, the steps to heal and recover began.

    The key for me was to become more independent. I got an apartment and for the first time, I was living alone. I can't describe how great it felt to come home after work and relax. I paid my own bills, did my own taxes, and lived independently. I took control of my own life. For the first time, I felt like a real man. I dictated what was for dinner, what décor was in the apartment, and I didn't answer to anyone. I learned from that experience that life will always throw difficult and sometimes depressing situations at you, but you have to quickly heal and recover. You can't allow yourself to stay in that place, because if you do, you'll never get out.

I've always been the guy that makes everyone laugh. Even when I was depressed, I made everyone else happy. I never showed anyone what was really going on with me. I would crack jokes, be the life of the party, then go home and break down.

When you feel yourself getting down about something, don't stay there. In this life you have to keep moving forward. If you stop, you'll be stuck in quicksand.

You have the same superpower I do. You can heal and recover from anything that's thrown at you. It's easier said than done, but you can do it. Life isn't set up for you to fail; it's set up for you to win. Don't let things that you can't control take control of you. If you want to live your best life: heal and recover. If you stay in a dark place too long, you're not going to find your way out. I know this from experience. Remember: there's always someone that has a worse situation than you. I'll bet if you thought about it, there's at least one person you know that you would never want to trade places with. We spend too much time stressing over things from our past, and situations we can't control. How many times have you or someone you know lost sleep while worrying about whether or not they were going to keep their job? How many times have you stressed yourself out over something when you had no control over the outcome? You have to get to a point where things roll off of you. The major disappointments and losses you're going to feel, but you have to get to a place where they don't drag you down into that dark place. You have a lot more living to do. Keep it pushing fellow hero, a better life awaits.

Are You Ready To Unleash?

In this thing we call life we are constantly trying to gain wisdom and knowledge about ourselves and others and I believe that the more we learn about each other and the more we gain understanding about our strengths and our weaknesses, the better we are in working together.

So many times, I see people hate on someone else's strengths and use their weaknesses against them. Remember, in doing that to others, you are making your own vulnerabilities known. It is not just important to know what our strengths and weaknesses are, but it is what we do with that knowledge that exposes our true selves. Learning more about yourself is not just a gift to you, it is a gift to others. Knowing yourself and being your powerful self helps you to empower others using your gifts. I hope that in reading this book it has helped you to gain a better understanding of how to discover, accept and embrace all that you are and what powers you hold within. When we unite as a team and use our superpowers for good, the world becomes a more peaceful place.

The co-authors of this book took a deep look into what life has brought them to and through, along with the lessons learned on the journey. The transparency that they share in their stories shows that at least one of their superpowers has to be courage. It takes major courage to open your life up and show how things that they viewed as challenges, detours, and distractions were turned into motivation toward change and growth. They have taken on a huge responsibility. Let's create our own metropolis and work together to make this world a better place to live, raise children, grow relationships and just BE IN!

So, grab your capes and join us on this journey of discovery, there is a seat waiting for you at the table of Super Heroes!

Call Your Power Back!
IT'S TIME TO UNLEASH!

List of things that you like about you! (Strengths)

1. _____
2. _____
3. _____
4. _____
5. _____
6. _____
7. _____
8. _____
9. _____
10. _____

List of things you could work on about yourself (Weaknesses)

1. _____

2. _____

3. _____

4. _____

5. _____

6. _____

7. _____

8. _____

9. _____

10. _____

Questions to ask yourself when discovering and accepting your Superpowers:

What is my Superpower?

_____
_____
_____

What are my weaknesses? (Think Kryptonite)

_____
_____
_____
_____

What challenges might I face as I embrace my superpower?

_____
_____
_____
_____

Known for her wit, candor and her passion, Lisa Dove Washington is a wanted speaker, interviewer and event host. As a magazine publisher and a DC native, Lisa has a connection to the local community that many rival. Whether she's volunteering with a young girl mentorship program or hosting a product launch party with DC finest, Lisa's gift to gab and contagious energy sets the mood of the room. Proud graduate of Howard D. Woodson Sr. High School, Lisa and her family support educational and social activities throughout the DMV. Currently, Lisa is using her communications skills that she gained from Spelman College to co-host an internet radio show, Girls Gabbin' airing on WIINDC.com. To learn more about Lisa's upcoming schedule and her new book, The Power of Shut Up, check out lisadovewashington.com. To book Lisa for your next event, visit the contact us link on her website.

Signature Speaking Topics

- Share the Shine – Stop holding your gifts hostage, they were given to you so you can share them with the world!
- Women O Women – Women need to know that we are so much more powerful when we work together. United WE are an Unstoppable Force!
- Our Youth or Our Future; Invest in them. We need them just as much as they need us so let's support each other and close those generational gaps
- The Power of Shut Up – Learning how to "Tame the Tongue" is necessary! What you say, how you say it, when you say and if are all factors in communicating effectively. Kids, Adults, Employers/Employees Husbands/Wives and Teens can all communicate better by learning the shut-up power.

Social Media Contact Info:
Website: www.lisadovewashington.com
FB: @LisaDoveWashingtonLLC
Twitter: @LWashingtonCCM
Instagram: @mrsldwashington

LISA DOVE WASHINGTON
RADIO SHOW CO-HOST/BEST SELLING AUTHOR/
FOUNDER OF DOVE STYLE MAGAZINE/
CEO OF TOUCHED BY A DOVE (CRAFTS)/
FOUNDER OF TOUCHED BY A DOVE PUBLISHING

Touched by a Dove is a business that makes handcrafted home and office décor such as wreaths, wall art, pillows, purses, etc. All crafts are handcrafted w/ lots of love. Check out the wonderful creations by Touched by a Dove by visiting Touched by a Dove pages on:

Facebook

Instagram

Pinterest

Lisa Dove Washington is part of a duo along with Andrea Riley who are the dynamic ladies who co-host the GIRLS GABBIN' RADIO SHOW. They are two motivated and creative women who decided to collaborate and provide a platform to showcase the talents, visions and dreams. These two women have their own journeys separately but they decided to enhance the journey by joining together & "Sharing the SHINE"!

GIRLS GABBIN' is making their mark in the community!
- ➤ Tune In @ www.windcradio.com & find out more about these ladies & how they show up, lift up & EMPOWER others.
- ➤ If you are interested in being a guest on the Girls Gabbin' Radio Show, contact us @ www.girlsgabbin.com

"Shut Up!" I can imagine the look on your face when someone said those words to you. I'm sure your head spun around as you thought, Who are you talking to? As rude as those words are, sometimes they need to be heard. The Power of Shut Up offers a different perspective on these words and shows you how to embrace the power of listening and then respond while demonstrating maturity. It will cultivate new levels of authenticity and greater resilience, along with renewed peace and joy within you.

The Motivation behind "Unleash Your Superpower" collaboration book:

Unleash Your Superpower, 6: extraordinary stories about discovering and accepting the power within!

Where did the concept of Unleashing Your Power come from? Did I just pull that out of thin air? Not even close. It all started with my very first book that was just released April 21, 2019! This book was the catalyst for so many things and it is just the beginning of many things to come.

I always wanted to write my own book, and there were many, many ideas continuously swirling around in my head almost daily on what my book would be about, but I always believe that timing is EVERYTHING!

Life is a story in itself, and as we move through life we learn, we love, and we live. I have always been someone who loves to learn more, not just about other things, but more about me. One of the biggest things that I learned in my first 50 years of life was learning how to shut my mouth sometimes and the rewards were amazing. So amazing that I decided that I must share the knowledge and the experience so that others can witness and experience the rewards as well. I reached out to a friend to discuss possibly joining a collaboration book and during that conversation she asked me that question that I had been asked so many times before, "When are you going to write your own book?" That was the million-dollar question that I not only never had an answer to but the one question that caused me anxiety because it was the very thing that I wanted but also the thing that scared me the most. Who would read a book by me? Who cared what I would have to say? Where do I start and what do I do? Will the book do well? There were more roadblocks popping up in my head but that would be a whole other book, lol,

At that very moment after I ran a whole book of questions that would deter or defer my response, One thought popped into my head that was, "None of that matters and this is what I want to do so shut up and DO IT "!

And what better topic that the one thing I learned that had changed my life for the better? "The Power of Shut Up"! Before the phone call ended, my response to her was, "Let's Do It!" and the journey began. Not only was a part of the collaboration project she was offering, I was now on my way to writing my own book, something I had talked about doing for over 30 years. God's Timing is Mind Blowing.

Being an English Major/Communication Minor at Spelman College, communication has always been important to me. Communication is necessary in absolutely everything that you do in life, but more importantly is how you do it and when you do it so and the decisions you make regarding that can shape and mold everything that happens in your life. I had experienced this in some heartbreaking ways and knew that I still had a lot to learn.

My journey to discovering the Power of Shut Up was not an easy one but what I gained from learning it was that, what you say, how you say it, when you say it and the decision to say it can make a break your relationship, your friends, your job, your business and sometimes even your life! Those were all the things that meant everything to me so why not do everything I can to make sure I am making the right decisions so that I protect all of it. "The Power of Shut Up" was born and not only did it teach me some amazing life lessons, I was also excited that now others would be able to do the same thing.

Excerpt from the Power of Shut Up

"Mastering this concept requires both a process and a practice that will be taught throughout this book through coaching, practical tips, and guided conversations. The Power of Shut Up will help you dig into your inner thoughts and discover why being heard is such a great accomplishment, but why listening can save you from unnecessary chaos. As you go through life, interacting with others, sharing your opinions, and making decisions, this book will help you think before you speak, but most importantly, think before you react."

But why stop there? What if there were other powers that we could learn, gain or discover that could help us to live better, be happier and love more? Then the swirling ideas started again. This is where "The Power of Shut Up" showed up in a grand way and started a flow of "firsts" and more "power", I'll be happy to explain!

The journey to discovering and accepting the power of shutting up was so rewarding and life-changing that I thought to myself, I can't possibly be alone in this journey. I also wanted others to explain the Unleashing that I did in the process so not only had a released my very first book, The Power of Shut Up, I discovered that now only had I found my personal power, I had found my lane, my niche', my path. About 2 months later, I launched my very own publishing company, Touched by a Dove Publishing.

But I didn't waste anytime getting started on my very first publication under my new publishing company and what better way to keep the power fueled up, so I decided to publish my very first collaboration project and I wanted to gather up more super heroes and share the shine. There are many superpowers (gifts) waiting to be discovered, so I put out a call to action for people who were interested in sharing their journeys of discovery while being transparent about what the consequences, and difficulties were and combining them into a book that could be shared with the world. At that moment, the Unleash Your Superpower collaboration book was born!

I am honored to have worked with some great people who truly put their everything in to helping others discover and accept their Superpowers but being transparent and honest about what they experienced and learned. We are creating a metropolis that will help to make this world a happier place by knowing who we are and working to make sure we are showing up in a great way.

It's time for you to get it together and…………………………..

CALL BACK YOUR SUPERPOWER!

My Gratitude to You!

Shawn, I don't think there is enough space to express how grateful I am to have a friend like you in my life. Thank you for always having my back every time I have a "New Idea"! No matter how crazy it was, you were down for the cause. I have learned so much from you as a creative and because of a lack of better words, I continue to say, "THANK YOU FOR BEING YOU"

Charron, you have truly been a blessing to me. You have helped me to find my lane and pushed me walk in my purpose. You selflessly shared your gifts and for that you will always be blessed. I appreciate you more than you know and I am forever grateful for your faith and trust in me. From the bottom of my heart, Thank You!

Thanks to everyone who has ever supported any of my dreams. Your support was a driving force that has helped me in ways I can't even fully explain. I credit all of your love, kindness, faith and support for allowing me to say, "My Dreams came true" THANK YOU!

Lord, Thank you for the vision, the strength, the motivation and the faith to believe that I do could do it! I DID IT and I know without a doubt that I couldn't do it without you! I am using the gifts you gave me to give back!

"I can do all things through Christ which strengtheneth me."
Phillippians 4:13

www.ingramcontent.com/pod-product-compliance
Lightning Source LLC
Chambersburg PA
CBHW062023290426
44108CB00024B/2755